ONE HUNDRED

Secret Thoughts Cats Have About Humans

ALSO BY CELIA HADDON

One Hundred Ways for a Cat to
Find Its Inner Kitten

One Hundred Ways for a Cat to
Train Its Human

One Hundred Ways to a Happy Cat

One Hundred Ways to Be Happy

One Hundred Ways to Comfort

One Hundred Ways to Friendship

One Hundred Ways to Say I Love You

One Hundred Ways to Say Thank You

One Hundred Ways to Serenity

ONE HUNDRED

Secret Thoughts Cats Have About Humans

BY

Celia Haddon

ILLUSTRATIONS BY

Jilly Wilkinson

Hodder & Stoughton
LONDON   SYDNEY   AUCKLAND

British Library Cataloguing in Publication Data
A record for this book is available from
the British Library

ISBN 0 340 86170 3

Printed and bound in Great Britain by
Bookmarque Ltd, Croydon, Surrey

The paper and board used in this paperback are natural
recyclable products made from wood grown in sustainable
forests. The manufacturing processes conform to the
environmental regulations of the country of origin.

Hodder & Stoughton
A Division of Hodder Headline Ltd
338 Euston Road
London NW1 3BH
www.madaboutbooks.com

Contents

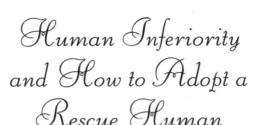

Human Inferiority and How to Adopt a Rescue Human

Humans actually believe that they are the superior species. This delusion explains many of the silly human behaviours that are so frustrating for us. Some of our best friends are humans, but, let's face it, as a species they are very limited.

Humans are pack animals like dogs – emotionally needy creatures that can't manage without a social group. In any group all humans need a leader – another way of saying that they need a cat to look up to.

Despite the overwhelming evidence to the contrary, humans still think they domesticated us, when it's obvious that we domesticated them. They are often maladroit and clumsy in carrying out our wishes, but they make very good domestic pets, once they are properly trained.

Adopt a rescue human. They think they are adopting you. Humans that need homes go to special places where cats are kept. These are rescue humans.

If you are in one of these adoption centres, a stream of stray humans will pass by you. When you see one you like the look of, you can go to the end of your run, rub against it and make chirruping noises. Humans that respond immediately will make good pets.

Beware of cat addicts. For them, one cat leads to another, and another, and another ... They fill their homes with cats, sometimes 30 to 40 at a time. It's hell inside, like living in an overcrowded hostel with nowhere to retreat to away from the others. These compulsive cat collectors don't have the money for decent cuisine or veterinary care. If you have to move in for a time, move out again as soon as possible.

Gay tom humans and female singles make the best pets of all. They can be absolute treasures in the home and there's less chance of your relationship being ruined by the arrival of human kittens.

Stray humans often include those with behaviour problems, which is why a previous cat left home. These problems are difficult to spot until you have moved in. A course of obedience training will usually help but there's no need to work yourself to death trying to make your human an acceptable pet. After all, you can always get a new one.

There is one kind of human that is always, unvaryingly cruel. It is called the 'vet' and it wears a white coat. It enjoys stabbing needles into cats. It opens our mouths and peers inside. It smells disgusting – of chemicals and animal pain. There are dreadful dogs waiting with us – panting and barking with stress and fear. It is a terrible place, a kind of torture room for animals.

Be cautious about humans that keep dogs. Do you want to mix with a mere dog? Dogs look up to humans. We cats look down on humans. So we also look down on the dogs for looking up to them.

A note of caution in your new home. It used to be thought that tom humans were leaders within the human family. But further research has shown that the real leader of the household – after you, of course – is the female human.

Stay away from 'breeders'. They often don't breed themselves, they breed by proxy – through us. Few of them have pedigrees, so they have invented a feline class system. Instead of love matches (oh, those wonderful nights on the tiles!) they force us into arranged liaisons by shutting us females up in a tiny cat chalet with a tom that is often kept as a life prisoner inside.

The same cat snobs, who enjoy showing off what beautiful cats they have, force us cats to sit in cages for hours and hours at a time in a church hall or some such draughty place. It's deadly boring. Remember, pedigrees are purely for human, not feline, pleasure.

There's a strange attraction about humans that hate cats. Perhaps it is the lure of reforming them. Their body language, their reluctance to pet us and the way they move away turns us on. But don't be tempted by a relationship with a cat hater – it's not worth it.

The Dysfunctional Species — Bald, Nearly Blind, with Only Two Legs

Human beings have two legs instead of the normal four. They can stand on their own two feet but they are easily unbalanced. This is quite useful if you are running away with a bit of skin off the turkey. Run through their legs.

21

Humans are diurnal, which means that they sleep at the wrong time of the 24-hour cycle and they have no idea of the importance of dawn. If you decide to take a human as a pet, you can try to train them in dawn-waking by jumping games at 3 a.m.

Humans waste energy fecklessly, unlike we cats who spend quality time conserving energy. They rush around doing pointless activities like work, shopping and cooking, instead of simplifying their lives into energy intake (snack), energy conservation (catnap), energy restoration (snack again), more energy conservation for digestion (catnap again) and so on.

Human eyesight is poor. It's pitiful to see them blundering about, stubbing their toes in the dark, but their blindness is useful if you decide to snack on the hamster at midnight.

They are mostly bald. They have a little hair in the wrong places – often the sweaty bits, just the places where we have less hair.

Tom humans suffer from alopecia on their head. The hair seems to fall off with age. This looks like a symptom of disease but it is part of the normal human ageing process.

The females seem to want to be even balder than they already are. They hate even the small amount of fur that they have. They groom it off their legs and under their arms. Weird or what?

Probably because they are embarrassed by their baldness, humans put layer after layer of 'clothes' on themselves to cover their nakedness. They change these substitutes daily. It's pathetic to see them worrying about what to put on to cover up their skin problem.

Caring and conscientious cats often try to cure human baldness by relocating some of their own fur on their human. If you decide to do this, you will achieve maximum effect by rubbing your light fur on to their dark clothing or your dark fur on to their light clothing. But it's a thankless task, because humans don't do gratitude.

Human kittens have no whiskers at all. Even the tom human whiskers are odd – very bushy and not much use as space and direction finders. They don't vibrate like ours do.

In one of the most stupid human behaviours, many tom humans go in for daily self-mutilation, cutting off their whiskers so that their cheeks are unnaturally bald. Ugggh, how could they? A cat's whiskers are its pride and joy.

Some human toms cut off the hair that grows out of their ears. Yet they like the hair in our ears and often say that it looks really pretty. Why don't they like hair in their own ears?

Their claws are very wide and soft, and useless for territory marking. We have to scratch the furniture and the carpet for them. For some reason this act of kindness upsets them mightily – probably because it makes them feel their unfortunate inferiority. Some respond by throwing things.

If Only They Could Speak ...

Some humans understand almost everything we are saying. To us they may seem just like dumb animals, but they are cleverer than we think. They seem to have some kind of primitive vocal language of their own.

We can hear a mouse's footfall, but humans have such poor hearing, they can't even hear us coming.

They cannot keep quiet and listen. They repeatedly vocalise to us almost as if they were trying to talk to us.

Humans have never mastered cat calls. The real suckers make idiotic attempts to chirrup back at us or even to meow. They vocalise stuff like 'Puss, puss, puss'. They may also use a call noise peculiar to you, like 'Sam' or 'Mog'. They have the illusion that we are like dogs and will come when called. Do not respond. It just gives them ideas above their station.

Humans can't caterwaul –
except in the bath or sometimes when they play the piano.

Because their vocal repertoire
is so inadequate, they listen
to artificial caterwauls from boxes
called radios, music players and
TVs. You must learn to tune out
this noise, just as you have tuned
out the calling vocalisations.

Human beings snore so loudly that it's often hard for a cat to get a decent night's sleep. The noise can be reduced if you get inside the bed under the duvet. If all else fails, claw them awake.

There's a noise that humans call 'laughter'. It consists of a kind of yodelling noise with a heaving chest. The significance of this vocalisation remains a mystery, particularly when it is elicited by our normal and sensible behaviour. At such moments a cat has to rise above natural anger and try to feel compassion for its dysfunctional human.

Their disabilities – no tail, ears that won't move and a fixed upright position – mean that their body language vocabulary is small.

They can't even puff out their fur to make themselves look bigger, because they have so little. They claim that the hair of their head 'stands on end' but it doesn't. It's too limp and floppy. So another way of expressing themselves in articulate body language is lost.

They cannot purr. Cat psychologists suggest that this gap in the human vocal repertoire is due to their lack of inner confidence and serenity.

Why Can't They Wash Properly?

Humans sweat all over. We only sweat through our paws. Their top paws do get hot and sweaty but so do their arms, their legs, their tummies, their backs, their bottoms – and so on. They are so embarrassed by this that they cover up their own smell with artificial smells (can you believe it?).

Humans can't wash themselves properly. Their tongues are too smooth and too floppy – hopeless for cleaning. And they are too stiff and disabled to reach the specially messy bits.

Caring cats sometimes try to give their human a good wash. But it's a massive job (they have so much bald skin) and humans wriggle and try to run away. Don't expect any thanks.

To get clean, humans fling themselves into a water container and loll about in their own dirty water. Most of us keep well clear of this deranged activity, though the more daring among us enjoy sitting on the edge of the bath and marvelling at the bizarre baldness of the human body.

No cat has succeeded in housetraining a human to the litter tray. Humans have the digging instinct, but somehow this no longer connects with the elimination instinct. Outside, humans sometimes dig into the soil as if they were going to dispose of their mess in a decent feline fashion. Instead they create a purrfect soil latrine and don't use it. Then they get upset when we do!

The human substitute for an indoor litter tray is a Big White Drinking Bowl called a toilet. They sit on it or spray into it from a standing position.

There are strange human rituals about the seating device on top of the toilet. Years of feline observation and research have failed to understand the significance of whether the seat is up or down. Toilet seat habits are inexplicable but make some humans very angry with each other.

Humans use the same indoor room for both cleaning and toilet – another disgusting human habit. It is as if we cats sat near the litter tray when having a proper wash – which, of course, we never do. Only a truly dysfunctional species would wash itself in the same place that it used for elimination.

The Big White Drinking Bowl, which they use as a latrine, can be used by athletic cats wanting a drink. But it is easier to use the water fountain, which is placed over a Smaller Drinking Bowl at a greater height. There is a similar bowl in the kitchen, also with a sort of drinking fountain. A tap switches the fountain on and off. But be warned, one fountain can be very hot.

Most humans do not usually spray outside the bowl. But some tom humans go into the garden late at night and deliberately mark their territory by spraying. This may be a sign of territorial insecurity.

They'd Be So Much Happier Neutered or Spayed!

Human sex and reproduction is bizarre. They are ready to mate day in and day out. There's no proper time or season. No other animal behaves in this promiscuous way but it's important for a cat not to be judgemental. They really can't help it.

They would be so much happier neutered or spayed by a vet. Then there would be no need for them to chase after other humans. Instead they could concentrate on having a loving relationship with their cat. If only we could do it to them, before they did it to us!

Young tom humans occasionally behave like we do. They roam around making a nuisance of themselves, looking for sex and getting into fights.

Even mated tom humans sometimes stay out all night and don't come when called. This makes human females angry. But they don't seem to mind the same behaviour in us cats. Purrhaps it is just our supurrior charm.

Humans suffer from low fertility. A female usually gives birth to only a single kitten, or 'baby', as it is known. A proper litter of several human kittens is rare.

Human kittens often don't have anyone of their own age to play with, but it doesn't matter as much as it would for one of our kittens, as they are amazingly retarded.

Instead of a neat row of nipples either side of the tummy to feed a litter of kittens, the human female has only two nipples. This may explain why many of them are incapable of suckling their young.

The low nipple count may explain obsessive fixation on nipples by some human males in search of sex. We are a decent species and would never confuse the symbols of kitten feeding with sexual desire! But, oh dear, humans!

It takes several weeks before human kittens start to go on four legs like nature intended. But, at about a year old, they start using only their hind legs in an evolutionary quirk. Our kittens walk only a few days after birth – another obvious reason why cats arc the superior species.

The human ability to pick up housetraining is also chronically slow. It can take several years before a human kitten is reliably dry at both day and night. We cats pick this up in a matter of weeks.

A Genetic Inability to Mouse and Other Eating Disorders

Most humans would starve in the wild. They can't mouse.

They ruin meat. Only a small minority, the most sophisticated humans, have the good taste to eat it raw like we do. The restaurants that serve raw meat to their humans are the very expensive ones.

For hundreds of years, caring cats have tried to teach their humans to eat mice. They have brought back delicious dead mice, and, with enormous self-control, have not eaten them but given these little delicacies to their humans. Humans don't eat

them. They never eat them. Not
even the tiniest nibble. This is a
severe disorder of the predatory
instinct.

Worse still, when we self-lessly bring home living mice, especially to teach our dumb humans how to hunt, what do they do? These large and powerful animals run away from the smallest mouse! Some scream out loud or jump on chairs.

The human equivalent of mousing is something called shopping. Humans go out and hunt down tins and bags of food, bringing it back for consumption in the safety of their home.

Luckily, although they cannot be trained to eat mice, they can be trained to bring back the right brand of cat food. Set up a shopping obedience programme with the help of the manual *One Hundred Ways for a Cat to Train Its Human*.

Humans expect us cats to eat the same tinned food or dry biscuits while they dine lavishly on fresh meat and fish. Some of them refuse to share, even when we get up on the table and sit close to the plate.

In a purrfect world there would be micecream for cats, not just ice cream for humans. But ice cream tastes quite good. If you can, purrsuade your human to give you some.

Naturally, when we have eaten, we wash up, cleaning our own dishes. They can't do this (those pathetic floppy tongues of theirs!). They don't even lick the plate to finish up the food. They have to plunge the dishes in water or use a noisy machine.

Wasteful humans throw away a lot of delicious food either into a small bin in the house or into a bigger bin outside. It's always worth pulling down the indoor trashcan and inspecting its contents. Outdoors there is more competition – from foxes, stray dogs and stray cats. Though humans don't want this food, they don't like us getting it either – selfish beasts.

Human Catnip and Other Compulsions

Human beings have several versions of catnip – a liquid form called alcohol, round tablets called pills, various white powders that they sniff or heat up, and even weird dried plants that they set fire to and smoke.

Just like us cats on catnip, drunk or stoned humans roll around making silly noises and behaving in an infantile fashion. We are recreational drug users – we use catnip for a bit, then walk away. But, unlike us, many humans don't know when to stop.

Possibly because they can't lap, humans have to throw alcoholic drinks down their throat using their paws. They are so stupid that they make themselves ill with drinking too much. Don't believe me? Then try purring in the ear of a human who was out late last night and see what happens – get ready for a rapid retreat!

Adisorder of the hunting instinct makes humans into
compulsive shoppers. This is found
most often in indoor humans who
don't have enough to do, rather
than in outdoor humans, the sort
that go out every day for work.
Compulsive shoppers bring home
innumerable items. Purrhaps the
single greatest difference between
our species is their senseless
obsession with collecting and stor-
ing things that are useless for
eating or playing with.

Compulsive overeaters exist among humans as well as cats. Just like greedy cats they develop large love handles and saggy tummy syndrome. There's an unfair phrase, 'fat cats', which means greedy humans, but it's about money, whatever that is, not food.

Humans are also fixated on small mouse tracks found on paper and mewsprint. For some reason humans always pretend that the tracks lead right under where we are sitting. Mewspapers should be used for playing crackle games, not for just gazing upon!

Another human compulsive habit is the TV. They are great watchers of wildlife, but they prefer the unreal version in a small square box in the living room. Most of them don't go out and watch the real thing.

This obsessive watching also occurs near another screen, called a computer, which has something called a 'mouse' attached to it by a string resembling a plastic tail. They scrabble with their fingers and move the 'mouse'

72

around on a small mat. If only we could teach them to hunt real mice, they'd spend less time with this artificial 'mouse'. If you press the delete button, you may be able to interrupt this unhealthy behaviour.

Finally, there is a plastic, rectangular item. It makes a repetitive trilling noise rather like a bird or an agonised kitten. Humans vocalise obsessively into these things. What is odd is that these things seem to vocalise back. Try meowing into it to drown out its noise.

Humans show affection to us by grooming with their fingers. They call it 'petting', because they are our pets. Do they understand the social significance of grooming – that the inferior animal, in this case the human, grooms the superior, in this case the cat?

Human affection may become human harassment. There are emotionally needy humans who spend their time trying to kiss us and pet us, even when we make it plain we don't want it.

They force their attentions on us. This inter-species harassment is abuse. Walk away from it with dignity.

Human Selfishness and Poor Service

Why do humans take up so much room on the bed? Even though they often have a spare bed or a sofa downstairs, they insist on sleeping with us in the main bedroom. And they seem to think it is all right to hog the bed. I suppose it is a touching display of their affection but sometimes, when they don't leave you enough space, it can be very irritating.

They make restless bedfellows – tossing and turning all through the night so that a cat can't get a decent night's rest. Worst of all, they do their mating inside the bed instead of on the rooftops. Sleeping between them will usually put a stop to this. All's fur in love and war.

They seem to have the idea that one or twice in every seven days they can just lie in late in bed – instead of getting up and preparing our breakfast at the correct time. They call it weekends, but we know that that's just an excuse for poor service.

Some thoughtful humans build us day beds high up on a shelf. They line them regularly with clean sheets and pillowcases, and supply a special boiler for warmth. The combination of fresh laundry and the heat is particularly relaxing.

Humans keep buying us beds – miserable small things that they place on the floor. They actually expect us to use new ones that smell of a shop. And, by the time the bed smells right, which takes several months, they take them away to give to the local rescue centre. Could anything be more maddening?

Humans are totally inconsiderate about chairs. They will keep turning us off our special chair. Establish control by the rule of claw!

There is only one area in which humans are our superiors – human flaps, which they call doors. These are similar to catflaps, only much larger and with the hinge on the side instead of at the top. Humans, with their brute strength, can open them. We can't.

Any normal feline wants to be able to establish the right to both indoor and outdoor territory. Doors are barriers to this. In summer, they are open, as they should be. But in winter, human beings keep trying to shut them. Worse still, they try to shut them on us when we are sitting in the doorway, contemplating the wider territory, and enjoying knowing that we could go out – or not – as the impulse takes us.

Why can't they stop the rain? They open the door and all this water is pouring down. Thoughtless of them.

There must be a better way than relying on humans to open and shut doors. But so far, the most intelligent feline brains have failed to come up with it. Nor has the combined intelligence of cats found a foolproof way of opening the door of the fridge. Luckily most of us can manage plastic shopping bags and egg boxes – so important for that stolen snack.

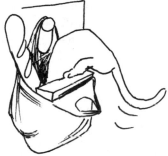

Common Problems with Pet Humans

Humans store small living fish in bowls or in garden ponds to keep them fresh, and they store small birds in cages, presumably to snack on them later. But they keep these food items for months and sometimes years. When we eat them, they get upset.

They also hang food containers in the garden to lure down birds for us. But they always seem to hang them too high up, so that we can't quite reach the birds. If we do make a kill, they try to take it away from us.

When we visit other humans for a second meal or a bit of extra admiration, they get jealous. Yet they often go into other people's homes or ask people back to our home – without so much as a by-your-leave. It's not fur play.

Spraying upsets humans really badly. They think we are being bad, when we are just making a cry for help.

Humans grow plants in the house. Obviously they are trying to provide green stuff and earth – which is really sweet of them. But then they get upset when we eat them or use the pot as a latrine.

When we jump on the table in front of their friends, they shoo us off. They don't mind us doing this when they're alone. Indeed we often sit on the table to watch them eat and most of our humans have no worries about eating the butter after we've had a lick or two. They just don't like us doing it in front of other humans!

If we clean our private parts in front of their friends, or use the litter tray in the kitchen when they are entertaining, they look embarrassed. Humans are just so prudish!

Sometimes they lie on the floor and do exercises rather like when we stretch. If we sit on their chest and look lovingly into their eyes, they don't respond very well.

For some reason when we take food out of the feeding dish, and put it on the floor to eat it where it tastes best, they get cross.

The females don't like it when we play with the little, jingling cat toys they wear in their ears. Why wear them if they don't want us to play with them?

Once a year they put a tree in the living room for a few days. Then they hang twinkling little balls from it. This tree is probably for us, since cats like climbing trees and they know we like twinkling balls. So we climb up the tree and we bat the little twinkling balls. When the tree falls down, they get upset. Forgive them – after all, it's Christmas.